Practical Pre-School

Exploring Emotions

Ros Bayley

Promoting emotional intelligence   2

Feeling happy   4

Feeling unhappy   6

Feeling afraid   8

Feeling angry   10

Feeling disappointed   12

Feeling guilty   14

Feeling jealous   16

Feeling lonely   18

Feeling excited   20

Feeling proud   22

Feeling irritable   24

Feeling hopeful   26

How to help your child handle their emotions – a page for parents   28

Published by Step Forward Publishing Limited
25 Cross Street, Leamington Spa CV32 4PX Tel: 01926 420046 www.practicalpreschool.com
© Step Forward Publishing Limited 2004   Illustrations: Cathy Hughes
All rights reserved. No part of this publication may be reproduced, stored in a retrieval system, or transmitted by any means, electronic, mechanical, photocopied or otherwise, without the prior permission of the publisher.

Exploring Emotions ISBN: 1 902438 84 1

EXPLORING EMOTIONS   1

Promoting emotional intelligence

Emotional intelligence may be even more important for children than academic achievement. If this is the case, it is really important that those who care for and educate children have a thorough understanding of what it is and how we can help children to develop it

The term 'emotional intelligence' was coined by two US psychologists, Peter Salovey and John Mayer. Put simply, an emotionally intelligent person:

- Is able to understand, express and manage their emotions
- Can read and understand the emotions of others
- Responds well to others and has the ability to get on with a wide range of people
- Has positive self-esteem and self-image
- Is comfortable with who they are
- Is usually easy to talk to
- Shows empathy for others
- Works well as part of a group
- Is optimistic and confident
- Has the emotional strength to deal with the ups and downs of daily life
- Has good interpersonal skills
- Sorts out problems in an assertive rather than an aggressive way
- Can think reflectively and make links between their actions and their emotions

'The more we learn about how the brain works, the more we begin to realise that effective learning depends on emotional energy.'

They are also able to delay their gratification, and this is important when you think how many things in life require hard work and determination. The fact that something may be worth waiting for does not mean that everyone can do it, but this is one of the key qualities that characterises an emotionally intelligent person.

The secret of success

Looked at in this way you can begin to see why these qualities are fundamental to success both at school and in life in general. In fact, academic achievement without emotional intelligence is not much use to anyone! Most of us know people who have achieved highly academically but are completely incapable of sorting out simple problems in daily life!

Daniel Goleman, who has spent many years researching emotional intelligence, says: 'People who cannot marshal some control over their emotional life fight inner battles that sabotage their ability for focused work and clear thought'.

Mind over matter?

The more we learn about how the brain works, the more we begin to realise that effective learning depends on emotional energy. As human beings, we are driven more by emotion than logic - it all depends on how we feel and how well we can manage those feelings.

In evolutionary terms, there was an emotional brain long before there was a rational one and this has had a profound effect on the way we function. Think for a moment about the last time you were 'full of feeling'. Maybe you were angry or upset about something, and the more intense these feelings became, the harder it became to think rationally. In such situations, our emotional brain overpowers our thinking brain, making rational thought difficult, and this is when we often do things that we later regret.

However, the higher our level of emotional intelligence, the greater our capacity for dealing with such situations. Emotional intelligence enables us to

EXPLORING EMOTIONS

function more effectively under stress and helps us not to lose our heads, and even when we do respond in a way that we later regret, we are much more likely to be able to sort our way out of the difficulties we find ourselves in.

Can it be taught?

Nobody can be emotionally intelligent all of the time. Our emotional state is constantly changing in response to the various situations in which we find ourselves, but in the light of what we know, two questions seem paramount: Is it possible to teach children to be more emotionally intelligent, and if it is, will this improve their learning and help them to be more successful in life? I think that the answer to both of these questions is a resounding 'yes' and would like to offer some suggestions for how this might be achieved in some key areas.

Understanding emotions

- Acknowledge and talk about children's feelings. This will help them to become increasingly able to identify and describe how they feel and lead to greater self-awareness.

- Value all of a child's emotions, including those that may be viewed as negative. Remember, all feelings are real for the person who is feeling them, and you can acknowledge someone's feelings without needing to agree with them!

- Be prepared to spend time with a child when they are sad, angry or fearful and try not to become impatient with the emotion.

- Respect the child's emotions and try not to make light of their negative feelings.

- Do not feel that you have to sort out every problem for a child.

Managing emotions

- Try to avoid telling children how you think they should feel.

- Listen with attention and empathise with how children are feeling.

- Offer guidance on how to regulate emotions, set limits, and help children to learn how to express emotions in a way that does not hurt others.

- Encourage them to think reflectively and learn from their mistakes.

- Provide a safe place where children can go when things get too much.

Self motivation

- Give children choices, encourage them to take on appropriate responsibilities and show confidence in their ability to succeed.

- Recognise and celebrate children's achievements.

- Make learning activities fun, varied and relevant.

- Help children to set targets for themselves. Discuss their aspirations with them and encourage them to aim high.

- Offer support when things go wrong and help children to see that making mistakes offers a valuable opportunity for learning.

- Consult with children about how things should happen and encourage them to offer their ideas. Help them to see that they can influence how things turn out.

- Create a culture where it is acceptable to take risks.

Understanding emotions in others

- Describe feelings when children are unkind or hurtful and make the most of disagreements, fights and conflicts as a vehicle for exploring emotions.

- Talk about the feelings of the characters you read about in stories or see on television or video.

- Encourage children to help others who are emotionally distressed.

- Teach them how to resolve conflicts, and help them to understand that we can disagree with someone and still like and respect them.

- Model emotionally intelligent behaviour.

Learning about relationships

- Play cooperative games and provide opportunities for children to work cooperatively.

- Help children to understand that when they are working as part of a group they have a personal responsibility to that group.

'When we have emotional intelligence we have the resilience to cope with whatever life throws at us.'

- Encourage them to understand that people who work well together are able to achieve more than people who do not.

- Model emotionally intelligent behaviour through your relationships with the children.

- Model emotionally intelligent behaviour in your relationships with other adults.

Skills for modern living

There's no real mystique to emotional intelligence - it's only what good parents and carers have always tried to develop in their children. However, it's perhaps more important today than it's ever been.

We live in a society that is changing at an unprecedented rate. The days of 'a job for life' are long gone. During someone's lifetime they may have to re-train several times, and this will call for adaptability and the ability to learn quickly and effectively.

In a densely populated world where life is lived in the fast lane, it is more difficult than ever before to feel a sense of identity and belonging, without which our lives will never feel fulfilled. Emotional intelligence will make the crucial difference. When we have emotional intelligence we have the resilience to cope with whatever life throws at us. We know that there is no such thing as failure, and we will try, try and try again until we reach a satisfactory outcome. We believe in ourselves and in our ability to succeed, and in an age of uncertainty, what could be more important than that?

Exploring emotions:
Feeling happy

Happy is a lovely emotion to explore, and as you do, you will inevitably talk about many other emotions and help to build that essential feelings vocabulary

If children are to become emotionally literate adults, able to understand and have mastery over their feelings, it is essential that this important work begins in the early years. It is a fundamental part of enabling children to be sensitive to the feelings of others, and in fact, a key element of all other emotional skills.

However, this awareness will not simply develop by chance. If children are to be aware of, and be able to talk about feelings, practitioners must provide them with the appropriate experiences. You must support children to recognise, name and acknowledge their feelings, and there are a wide variety of ways in which you can do that.

Teaching the 'tool words'
To talk about feelings you must have the necessary vocabulary, and because feelings are essentially abstract, one of the best times to develop this vocabulary with young children is when they are actually experiencing the feeling. If you can label feelings as they are happening, you build a bridge between the word and the feeling and make these abstract concepts much more easily understood.

So when you see children with big smiles on their faces, take a moment to comment on this and acknowledge what you have noticed with a 'You look happy today!' When children fall out over toys or friends you might say something like, 'You both look very cross.' When everyone does this on a consistent basis children soon build up an emotional vocabulary and will be able to tell you if you attach the incorrect label to what they are feeling. You can then enhance their understanding through a range of planned activities.

Family snapshots
Happy is perhaps one of the easiest of all the feelings to explore and children are quick to realise that happiness can mean different things to different people. They are also able to see that there are some things that make us all happy, and this activity is helpful in exploring similarities and differences. Ask children to bring a photograph from home that shows then doing something that has made them feel happy. Once they have shown their pictures to each other and talked about them, make a happy display. Talk about how they would like to caption their pictures and encourage them to look for similarities and differences.

A happy collage
Provide children with a variety of newspapers and magazines and get them searching for pictures of people who look happy. Talk with them about why they think the people look happy then let them cut the picture out and add it to a collection of pictures to make a happy collage.

Go on a happy walk
Walk around your local area and see if you can see anyone looking really happy. Encourage children to talk about why they think they are happy and keep a tally of how many happy people you can spot.

Make a happy diary
As children are playing, take some photographs of them when they are looking really happy. If you have a digital camera, print the photographs and show them to the children. Encourage them to talk about what they were doing at the time the photograph was taken and then collect the photographs in a diary. Let children decide how they should be captioned. Take photographs of the adults as well and add these to the happy diary.

Carry out a survey
Ask children to name one thing that, if they could do it right now, would make them feel really happy. With younger children give them the choice of several things and let them choose the one that would make them happiest. Use picture cards to help them decide. Once everyone has chosen, compare the results. Older children could graph the results on a chart.

Sing some happy songs
Encourage children to think of songs or pieces of music that make them feel happy.

Once you have compiled a list, have a happy concert. If the children find this difficult, make some suggestions of your own or present them with some alternatives to choose from.

Circle games
Make a circle of chairs for children to sit on and then pass around a 'talking object' such as a teddy. As each child gets the object, encourage them to say 'I feel happy when...'. Start by using this tag line yourself so that you can model how to do it. Once everyone has had a go, get the children to see if they can remember who said what.

Play 'Change seats'. For example, say to the children, 'If eating chocolate makes you happy, change seats', 'If riding on a bicycle makes you happy, change seats', 'If painting a picture makes you happy, change seats', and so on.

Using stories
Make a collection of stories which have really happy endings and play games with stories. For example, describe something that happened at the end of one of your stories and see if the children can guess which character or story you are referring to. You might say something like: 'This person was very happy because she would no longer have to do lots of horrible jobs or live with people who were not very nice to her. She would not have to wear rags. She would live in a castle and have nice clothes.'

Name a character and get the children to name something that made the character feel happy, for example 'The Billy Goats Gruff felt happy when...' or 'Little Bear felt happy when...'

Puppets and toys
Find an appealing soft toy and hide it in a bag or a box to add to the suspense. Explain to the children that you have a little friend who is feeling very unhappy. Slowly reveal your character to the children and encourage them to come up with reasons why they think he is unhappy. Once they have done this they can make suggestions for things they could do to make him feel happy. With older children you could use this scenario as a basis for a modelled or shared writing activity. They could make lists of things that might make your character happy, plan a party for him or write a story for him.

If you have any large puppets in your setting, create some scenarios where they are feeling really happy about something, or perhaps one where they enable someone else to feel happy. I have two puppets called George and Gloria, which I use for all sorts of scenarios. Here's one which you may like to try out. You can substitute the names of your own puppets.

The lost handbag
Optional resources/props: A handbag containing a scarf, a lipstick, a notebook with a shopping list in it, a purse and a key ring with a key on it.

George has had a new dragon kite and he insists on taking it out to fly it, even though there is not much wind. He and his mum go to call for Gloria and they drive to a place where there is a high hill. They really hope there will be enough wind to fly the kite, but unfortunately there isn't, so they decide to play on the grassy bank instead. They climb down a little way until they come to a flat part where there is some long grass.

While they are playing in the grass Gloria finds a handbag. They look inside and find a variety of things. Wondering what to do, they take it back to George's mum, who is waiting by the car at the top of the hill. She looks in the bag but there is no name and address anywhere. Then she notices a photograph of a black cat on a key ring. The cat looks like one that belongs to an old lady that she knows, so they all get in the car and drive to the house where the lady lives. When they show the bag to the old lady she is very, very happy. She had lost it when she was out walking her friend's dog!

Once you have shared this story with the children you can use it as a basis for discussion. Encourage them to think about how George and Gloria might have felt as a result of finding and returning the lady's handbag. Ask them if they can think of any occasions when something they have done has helped someone else to feel happy. Talk about the ways in which doing something for somebody else can make us happy.

Happy is a lovely emotion to explore, and as you do, you will inevitably talk about many other emotions and help to build that essential feelings vocabulary.

EXPLORING EMOTIONS

Exploring emotions:
Feeling unhappy

We need to be in touch with all feelings and negative emotions, although more difficult to manage, are just as important as positive ones and a natural part of being human

Scientists now understand enough about how the brain works to know that human behaviour is determined much more by the way we feel than by the way we think. The 'feeling brain' engages before the 'thinking brain,' and when feelings are running high it is not easy to think rationally.

The first and most important thing to remember is that all feelings are real for the person who is experiencing them. You may think that someone should or should not feel a certain way, but for the person concerned the feeling is a reality, and unless it is acknowledged it will only intensify. Acknowledging someone's feelings is a powerful way of helping them to return to a state of equilibrium. They feel listened to and experience our empathy, and this is important when children are feeling unhappy.

Faced with an unhappy child it is easy to feel slightly panicked and uncomfortable. You may feel an urge to distract the child and direct their attention to something more happy and enjoyable, but if you do this too quickly, you deny their feelings and rob them of a powerful learning experience. We need to be in touch with all our feelings, and negative emotions, although more difficult to manage, are just as important as positive ones. When negative emotions go unacknowledged, children begin to think that feeling that way is unacceptable, whereas what you need them to understand is that all feelings are real, and that experiencing negative feelings is all part of being human.

For very young children, learning about feelings happens most effectively in a real-life context. You can help unhappy children by acknowledging and labelling their feelings, by simply saying something like, 'You seem very unhappy today,' and offering comfort. If you get it wrong they'll soon tell you! This process enables them to identify what they are feeling and builds up their feelings vocabulary. It also puts them in a place where they can listen. Listening is almost impossible when you are flooded with feeling, so by taking children through this process and allowing them time to experience and come to terms with their unhappy feelings, you make it much easier for them to move on and begin to engage with the learning process. If not, their unhappy feelings may persist for much longer. Your sensitive acknowledgement helps them to begin to understand the power of their own emotions, and supports them to be able to read the feelings of others. This is the basis of emotional literacy.

You can develop this understanding further through building interesting and exciting activities into your weekly planning as well as providing them in response to issues that arise.

Stories and scenarios
One of the most powerful ways of helping children to explore feelings is through story, and if you want to really understand this power look no further than the massive popularity of soap operas. As adults observe the lives of the characters in these stories, they explore and validate their own emotions. So why not create soap operas for three- to five-year-olds?

All you need are some central characters, and these can be dolls, puppets or soft toys. Add to these a simple storyline and you have created a powerful context for learning. The soft toy characters will instantly engage the children at an emotional level, and when the emotions are engaged the learning is always deeper. You might like to try the following:

- Find a small soft toy or teddy bear and using a red felt pen make a mark on a piece of bandage (to look like blood) and bandage the toy's arm or leg. Put it in a box or a basket and cover it with a blanket (use a flannel or other small piece of material). Carry it into the room very, very carefully, explaining how you have found the little dog or teddy in the garden or playground and that it had fallen over. The children will identify with this scenario as most of them have experienced what it feels like for themselves. You can then discuss how your character may be feeling and generate ideas for how to help him begin to feel better. To give your storyline extra credibility, take a photograph of your toy in the place where you found him. This builds on the magic and enhances the emotional engagement. Encourage the children to share their own experiences of being upset. Older children could draw pictures of themselves and write sentences beginning with: 'I feel unhappy when…'

■ Look through magazines for pictures of people who look unhappy and talk about what you think is making them unhappy. Where appropriate, share your own experiences with them. When children spend time with emotionally literate adults they benefit hugely from such role modelling.

■ Develop further scenarios with your toy, for example bring him in holding something he is very pleased with, such as a toy or a balloon. On another occasion he can return looking unhappy because his balloon has burst or his toy has been lost. Here again, you will have created another valuable opportunity to talk about feeling unhappy. You will also be building the children's empathy skills and this is extremely important, for without empathy we cannot engage in moral reasoning.

■ When children are unhappy it is often a consequence of disputes with their peers, so if you have any large puppets in your setting, create a storyline that involves the interaction of two characters. (You could use dolls or teddy bears.) Create a scenario where one character won't share a toy with another or goes off to play with someone else, leaving the other one by themselves. You don't need to be a fantastic storyteller and your story does not need to be complicated. Once you have established the reason for your character's unhappiness the children can suggest ways in which the situation might be addressed.

■ Make the fullest possible use of published stories. There are some excellent ones about feeling unhappy, the most famous of which is possibly *Dogger* by Shirley Hughes. Dave, the central character, is inconsolable when Dogger, his much loved toy, goes missing, and when you share this story with children it provides a myriad of opportunities for discussing unhappiness and a wide range of associated feelings. Throughout the story Dave moves through feelings of sadness, anxiety, disappointment, frustration, excitement, relief and gratitude. With older children, make a picture map of the parts of the story when he is feeling these things.

■ Other excellent stories are *Billy's Sunflower* by Nicola Moon and *Danny's Duck* by Jane Crebbin, both of which are associated with unhappiness caused through the loss of something important. An added bonus of these two texts are the excellent illustrations, which depict the feelings of the characters with great power and sensitivity.

When discussing these stories with children, ask questions like:

'Can you think of some words that would describe how … is feeling?'

'Can you think of a time when you were unhappy because you lost something?'

(These questions can be applied to most stories when you are focusing on feelings.)

Useful resources
Storylines by Ros Bayley and Lynn Broadbent (Lawrence Educational Publications Tel: 01922 643833).

Ring of Confidence: A Quality Circle Time Programme to Support Personal Safety for the Foundation Stage by Penny Vine and Teresa Todd (Positive Press Tel: 01225 719204)

■ Create a feelings thermometer so that children can indicate in a concrete way how they are feeling on the continuum from unhappy to happy. This helps them to understand that feelings are not always totally polarised into happy and unhappy.

■ Talk about body language and what happens to our bodies when we are unhappy. Play some different kinds of music to the children and discuss how the music makes them feel. Once they have identified some music that makes them feel unhappy or sad, move around the room using sad body language. Then contrast with some happy music and movement.

■ Paint faces that are unhappy, and some that are happy. Talk about the ways in which they are different.

■ Use Persona dolls. These come without clothes or faces so that you can dress them yourself and give them any expressions you want.

Remember that feeling unhappy is a natural part of being human. We all feel unhappy some of the time, and we owe it to children to help them to understand this by allowing them to experience their unhappy feelings. The biggest favour we can do them is to be there with them, acknowledging their feelings and empathising with them. When we can do this we not only help them, but we also give them a model for helping others.

Exploring emotions:
Feeling afraid

You should always acknowledge children's fears as they experience them, but you can also develop their understanding of this painful emotion through a range of planned activities

Fear is a natural part of life, and something that young children experience in varying degrees. Our role lies in enabling them to understand that everyone is afraid sometimes and that being afraid is all part of being human. If we fail to do this, children's feelings of fear may be compounded by shame or guilt.

It is also important that we help children to see that fear can be a personal thing; that although some things may be frightening for everyone, different things frighten different people. Whilst one person may be fascinated by spiders, another may be terrified of finding one in the bath!

Activities that support children in understanding some of these complex issues can be beneficial and rewarding, but it is important to exercise great sensitivity.

When asking children to think about and talk about fear you may be focusing on things that cause them pain and discomfort, so it is really important to establish a climate of trust within which everyone can feel safe, and confident that they will not be laughed at.

The most important starting point is acknowledging children's fears as they experience them. If you can do this they will get the message that there is no shame in feeling afraid, understand that the feeling is something that happens to all of us and feel confident that they can look to you for help and support.

You can then develop their understanding of this sometimes difficult emotion through a range of planned activities. You might like to try out some of the following ideas.

Puppets, toys and dolls

Find a soft toy or teddy bear that looks appealing and will engage the children's emotions. Place your toy in a special box or basket and hide it under a towel or blanket. Explain to the children that there is someone who would really like to meet them but that he is too frightened to come out of the box. Ask them for their ideas about why he may be frightened and encourage them to suggest ways in which they could help him.

Once they have done this, let them try their ideas out. They usually have no difficulty coming up with ideas but if they do, support them by asking questions like: 'Do you think it would help if we all stayed very quiet and passed him round so that everyone could say hello and make friends with him?'

If you have any large puppets, create a scenario where one character frightens another. Children are always fascinated by props, so if you can bring credibility to your story by using some plastic snakes, spiders or stick insects, for example, so much the better.

Explain to the children that one character has been invited to stay at the other's house and that both of them are very excited about it. Build the story by talking about what they packed to take with them, the games they played and what they had for tea. (The children can help you build the story.) Then tell the children about how, when one character was cleaning their teeth in the bathroom, the other hid some toy spiders in the bed, and go on to explain that when they got into bed and saw the spiders they were so frightened they cried and cried to be taken home.

Encourage the children to talk about and name the feelings that were experienced by everyone concerned and consider how the story might have ended and how the parents might have felt.

This scenario works with most children in the Foundation Stage and, by the end of Reception, children are usually able to

8 EXPLORING EMOTIONS

discuss the issues with considerable complexity, and can even use the scenario as a basis for their writing.

Use the story as a springboard for discussing children's feelings. Talk about the things that frighten you, and let children add their own fears to the list. If appropriate, make a chart of all the different things that everyone is afraid of.

Stories and scenarios
Create further scenarios with your doll or puppet characters, for example the day one of them got lost in the supermarket or got locked in the toilet.

Tune into children's fears and, over time, explore them through simple story scenarios. Many children, for example, have experienced tremendous fear when they have become lost in a big store or on a beach. Have this happen to one of your characters and encourage children to generate strategies for helping. Encourage them to focus on what they would say to the character and the things they would suggest they do.

A visit to the dentist can be frightening for some children. Again, explore these feelings through your character and let the children make suggestions for how this situation can be handled.

Circle games
Play circle games that help children explore ideas about being afraid. You could collect pictures or make a list of some of the things that frighten the children, such as being in the dark, riding on a fast ride at the fair, being lost, climbing to the top of the slide, dogs, snakes or going to the dentist or doctors. Then play 'Change seats'.

Make a circle of chairs then go through your list and say, 'If you're frightened of spiders, change seats!' This is a concrete and practical way of helping young children to understand that people are all frightened by different things. With younger children, you can simply use your collection of pictures as a basis for conversations about feeling afraid. With older children, go round the circle with a tag line: 'I feel frightened when ….'

Fairy tales
Tell fairy tales which feature characters that are afraid, for example 'Little Red Riding Hood', 'Goldilocks', 'The Three Little Pigs', and talk about the feelings of the main characters, identifying the points in

the stories when they were frightened. With older children, read some of the more scary stories like 'Hansel and Gretel' and 'Jack and the Beanstalk'.

Story books
Use storybooks like *The Park in the Dark* by Martin Waddell, *A Dark, Dark Tale* by Ruth Brown, *The Bear Under the Stairs* by Helen Cooper and *'Can't You Sleep Little Bear?'* by Martin Waddell as a basis for discussion. For older children, the *Helping Hands* series published by Evans Brothers has some excellent titles that deal with fear. *'Could You Leave the Light On?'* is all about a little girl who is afraid of the dark and *'Mummy, Mummy Where Are You?'* deals with all the feelings associated with being lost.

Adult visitors
Invite adults into your setting to share their stories about when they have been frightened and talk with children about how they overcame their fears. This really helps children to understand that everyone feels frightened some of the time and enables them to see that fear is something that can be dealt with and worked through. It can also help them to begin to understand that fear has a positive side; that it can both help to keep us safe and help us to grow as human beings. Taking your driving test or parachuting from an aeroplane can be frightening but we can be extremely proud once we have done it successfully!

Props and role play
Create prop boxes and role-play situations that enable children to explore scary situations, for example a jungle expedition. Provide backpacks, binoculars, torches, sleeping bags, cameras, clothes to dress up in and pop-up tents. Make a place for the children to play in by draping blankets over a climbing frame, clothes' horse or table. Use a torch or battery-powered lantern and hold story-telling sessions in the dark, dark place. For a really scary experience, add cobwebs and bats and hang things from the roof to give the feel of a 'ghost train.'

Read and dramatise *'We're Going On A Bear Hunt'* by Michael Rosen and Helen Oxenbury. Explore the family's feelings at each stage of the story, allowing the children to sense the change in atmosphere when they discover the bear!

Play a game where everyone hides under the covers on a given signal. (The children can choose the things that they are going to be scared of!)

The beauty of all these activities is that they allow children to explore their fears in a safe context, to develop empathy for others who are afraid and begin to develop strategies for helping and supporting them. Carried out with thought and sensitivity, this work can really help young children to accept fear as something that is not only a natural part of life but something through which they can grow and develop as people.

Exploring emotions:
Feeling angry

Anger is a powerful emotion that can feel scary both for the person who is feeling it and for those who are witnessing it or on the receiving end! When someone is angry, we can all feel vulnerable

In our attempts to understand anger, or any strong emotion, it is useful to understand how the brain works. The limbic system (where the emotional brain is situated) will always have the capacity to over-ride the neo cortex (where the thinking brain is situated). In evolutionary terms, it was there first, and because the connections that run one way are much more powerful than those that run the other way, it is the feeling brain that 'kicks in' first. In other words, when we are full of feeling it is difficult to think, and never is this more true than when we are feeling angry!

So what are the implications of all this on our behaviour? Just think back to the last time you were really, really angry. The chances are that you did or said something that you later regretted. That's because you went straight from feeling to acting - without thinking.

Our job as practitioners is to help children learn to stop and think. We need to work with them to help them to understand that it's OK to be angry, that anger is a perfectly normal human emotion, and that what's important is that we try to express our anger in ways that do not hurt others. This is a tough but extremely important task, for anger is energy, and it has to go somewhere! Anger that is repressed can only 'go inside' and fester. Anger that is expressed thoughtlessly will nearly always end in aggression. However, with a consistent and systematic approach we can really help children learn to manage their anger effectively.

Using puppets and toys

Find a puppet or soft toy that will appeal to the children, and explain that he or she is feeling very angry. With the use of some simple props you can make the story come alive even more, for example have a broken toy or a ripped book or a burst balloon. If you have two puppets or toys, you can use one as the victim and the other as the perpetrator, but be careful that the aggressor is not always the same puppet or toy. This avoids any character being labelled as 'the naughty one', and helps children to understand that all of us can be naughty some of the time!

Ask children for ideas about what they think has happened and let the scenario unfold. You can bring the story to an end by incorporating their ideas about what they think should happen.

I have two puppets called George and Gloria, which I use for the following scenario about anger, and it never fails to grip the children and set the scene for some really good discussion. The children find it really easy to relate to George's

George is very angry

Gloria's grandad buys her a small present every week when he goes to the post offce to collect his pension. One day he comes back with a water pistol. Gloria has great fun playing with it in the garden and the next day she asks her mum if she can take it to nursery/school. Her mum says no and tells her to take it upstairs and put it in her toybox. Unfortunately, Gloria doesn't listen. She hides the water pistol in her bag and takes it to nursery/school.

That afternoon, during free play, George is painting a picture for his mum. He takes a lot of time and trouble over his painting and while he is doing it, Gloria sneaks her water pistol out of her bag and takes it to the washroom where she fills it with water. She squirts the walls, the door and the mirrors until all the water has gone!

As she is refilling the water pistol, she notices George who is just in the process of carrying his completed painting to the drying rack. Gloria rushes out of the washroom. 'George!' she cries, and pointing her water pistol at his painting proceeds to squirt it with water. As she does this, the paint runs, the paper tears and George breaks into floods of tears.

'Gloria,' he cries, 'I hate you and you're not my friend any more!'

Miss Gailey, their teacher arrives to see what the noise is about.

feelings and usually have plenty of ideas for how the story should end. It also helps to ask some good open-ended questions like:

- How do you think Miss Gailey will feel about what has happened?

- What do you think Gloria's mum will say when she finds out what has happened?

- Why do you think George feels so angry?

Once you have explored George's feelings you can introduce a further scenario where

10 EXPLORING EMOTIONS

the situation is reversed and George breaks one of Gloria's toys, or pushes her off a bike. This enables you to explore alternative ways of dealing with angry feelings. When you use these scenarios you really help children to think about and talk about feelings, and if you want to provide opportunities for further reflection you can use them as the basis for book-making. Reception class children will often use these scenarios as a basis for their own writing.

Using such scenarios gives children the opportunity to explore feelings of anger in a safe context when they are feeling calm, but you also need to think about how to deal with angry feelings as they happen throughout the daily routine, and this is when it is useful to know a little about conflict resolution.

Resolving conflicts and solving problems
When you are dealing with an angry outburst, the first thing you need to do is to acknowledge the feelings of all concerned, regardless of who is to blame. This not only helps everyone to calm down and puts them in a place where they can listen, it also helps to extend children's 'feelings vocabulary.' It is also important to decide whether to act immediately or whether it would be better to wait until everyone has cooled down.

Once everyone has calmed down you can begin to collect information about what has happened, and encourage children to express their feelings about the incident. You can then reflect this information back to all the children so that they can clarify, and if necessary, expand upon what has happened. The next stage involves you getting the children to come up with possible solutions together. Once this has happened you need to give follow-up support. When you support children to learn this process you make a real contribution to their emotional education and, at the same time, give them an important life skill.

Circle games
Make a circle of chairs and start a tag line, for example pass a teddy or 'talking object' around the circle and encourage the child who is holding the teddy to say, 'I feel angry when…' If the children can't think of anything to say, let them 'pass', and if they say the same as the person next to them don't worry too much.

The more you practise tag lines the better they'll get.

Collect some pictures of people who are looking angry. Pass the pictures around the circle and encourage children to offer their ideas about why the person is angry: 'I think this person is angry because…'

Using stories
Make a collection of stories about anger and share them with children. Use books like *Two Monsters* by David McKee and *Angry Arthur* by Satoshi Kitamura; use folk tales like 'The Three Little Pigs', 'The Billy Goats Gruff' and 'Jack and the Beanstalk', which all feature angry characters and provide opportunities for role play.

Share your experiences
Tell stories about things that have made you angry and encourage other adults to do the same. This really helps children to understand that everyone experiences angry feelings, and to see that even the adults they love and respect don't get it right all of the time!

Using your camera
Role play situations that make children angry and take photographs at various stages of the role play. For example:

Picture 1: Some children build a tower.

Picture 2: Some more children arrive and knock the tower down.

Picture 3: A pretend fight or argument.

The photographs can be used as a basis for discussion and the 'solution' can be photographed and added to the sequence.

Anger is not an easy emotion to handle, but by engaging in these sorts of activities you can help children to see that it is something that everyone feels, and that we all need to learn how to express strong feelings in ways that do not harm others.

Exploring emotions:
feeling disappointed

Even very young children will be familiar with what it feels like to be disappointed. They may not know what it is called, but they will certainly have experienced it

It can be difficult for young children to cope with looking forward to something and then finding out that it cannot happen. Really, really wanting something, and not being able to have it, can also be hard to handle.

As adults, we sometimes find it difficult to deal with children's feelings of disappointment, especially if we are the reason for that disappointment. We might try to distract children's attention and shift their focus to something else - which may or may not work! If it doesn't work, children's feelings may become even more extreme, for disappointment, just like every other feeling, requires our acknowledgement. When sensitively handled, children's feelings of disappointment can be used as a valuable opportunity for learning.

Using puppets and toys

If you have any large puppets, use them as characters within a simple story scenario through which the children can explore their feelings of disappointment. These scenarios do not have to be complicated. In fact, it is usually the simpler ones that work best. All you need to do is to think about the things that disappoint your children and then use those things as a basis for your story. For example:

- Have your characters looking forward to a trip to McDonalds (or somewhere similar). Maybe they are going to celebrate a birthday or meet some friends or relatives. Build the suspense and excitement by talking about how they are going to get there, what they want to eat, and then have them not able to go because the car has broken down or someone is ill.

- Your character could be about to have a birthday and have decided exactly what they want as a present, but when the big day comes, they do not get what they want. This works particularly well if you wrap up the present and let the children help your character unwrap it!

- Your characters could be about to go on holiday. They could have packed their suitcases and be ready to go, only to find out that the holiday has been cancelled because one of their parents (or themselves) becomes ill.

- Maybe your characters are going on a trip to the fair or theme park, but the trip is cancelled because of bad weather.

You will probably be able to think of many more suitable starting points. Once you have introduced the children to these scenarios you will find they have little difficulty relating to the feelings of the characters, and you now have a situation to which they can make a response. Encourage them to share their own experiences of times when they have felt disappointed and see if they can generate ideas for things that might make your characters feel a little bit better. For example, I was once working with some three- and four-year-olds on a scenario where the characters were disappointed because a picnic was rained off, and we all ended up having a picnic under a large table.

Such situations are excellent for exploring feelings and can also support children to think creatively. If you don't have any large puppets you can always use teddy bears or soft toys. With older children, these scenarios can also be used as a basis for writing experiences.

Using stories

There are many stories that can be used to explore disappointment, ranging from fairy tales, like 'Cinderella', to stories like Anthony Browne's *Gorilla* (Walker Books). In this story, the main character, Hannah, is often disappointed because her father is

The corner shop scenario

This short scenario provides a really good springboard for exploring feelings of disappointment.

Find a toy that will immediately capture the children's imaginations and would be something that they would really like to have for themselves. I use a little chimpanzee called Malcolm. I set the scene by telling them about a little girl called Gina, who goes into the corner shop each day on her way to nursery or school.

One day when she is in the shop she sees something that she has never seen before, and immediately wants it. By this time the children are really curious to know what it is, so very slowly I get the chimpanzee out of a box and let them stroke him. I explain how Gina asks how much the chimpanzee costs and how she decides that when she gets home from nursery/school, the first thing she is going to do is to count up her money to see if she has enough to buy him.

When Gina finds out that she doesn't have enough money she is very disappointed and asks her mum to help her to work out how much more she will need. Gina then begins to think about all the things she can do to get the money. She washes dishes, cleans the car and does lots of jobs for her grandma and grandad.

Each day on her way to nursery/school she goes into the shop to see the chimpanzee. She even gives him a name. She calls him Malcolm, and as she strokes his soft brown fur she explains that soon she is going to buy him and take him to live with all the other toys in her bedroom.

The days go by until eventually Gina has enough money to buy Malcolm. Feeling very happy, she takes all her money to the shop, only to find out that someone else has already bought him.

too busy to spend any time with her doing the things she wants to do.

For younger children, *Through my Window* by Tony Bradman and Eileen Browne (out of print - try your library) provides a good context for exploring feelings of disappointment. Another book that you may find useful is *Threadbear* by Nick Butterworth (Hodder Children's Books) and for older children, *Jamaica and Brianna* by Juanita Havill (Mammoth).

Playing circle games

A good game for exploring feelings of disappointment is the party game 'Pass the parcel.' Wrap up a parcel and play the game in the usual way, but use it as a context for exploring feelings. Ask the children:

■ What does it feel like when the music stops and you have got the parcel?

■ What does it feel like if you never get the parcel?

Make a circle of chairs and start a tag line, for example pass a teddy or a 'talking object' around the circle and encourage the child who is holding the teddy to say, 'I feel disappointed when...' If children can't think of anything to say, let them pass. With practice they'll soon get the hang of it!

Especially with older children, encourage them to see that we experience feelings of disappointment at different levels. A good activity to help with this is to think of several situations that would be disappointing and get children to order them from the least disappointing to the most disappointing. For example:

■ Missing a trip to the zoo because you are ill.

■ Dropping your ice cream on the pavement.

■ Being taken out to buy a pet and finding that the pet shop is closed.

This activity usually leads to some disagreement and this is useful as it helps the children to see that people

are affected differently and that sometimes, something that may be extremely disappointing for one person is not so disappointing for someone else.

Share your own experiences

Encourage the adults in your setting to tell stories about their disappointments. These could be the things that happened to them when they were children, or more recent disappointments. This process helps children to understand that disappointment is something that happens throughout our lives, and that there are some situations to which there is not a happy ending.

Ask children's parents and carers to share some of their disappointments. Make a book by having a photograph of the person concerned and then a statement that begins, 'I was disappointed when...' and ends with a short description of the event.

Get your camera out

Get everyone in your setting, adults included, to see if they can make a disappointed expression. Set the scene by telling a disappointing story and then snap people's expressions. Once you have processed the pictures, encourage the children to notice what happens to people's faces when they are disappointed. Use the photographs as a basis for a painting activity and make a gallery of disappointed expressions. Add some more paintings of situations where people are disappointed. Get children to look through magazines to see if they can find any pictures of people looking disappointed. Cut the pictures out and add them to your gallery.

Through carrying out these activities you can create a meaningful context in which the children can explore feelings of disappointment, and help them begin to understand that whilst these situations cannot always be resolved, there is no situation that cannot be improved by taking a positive view and engaging in a little creative thinking!

Exploring emotions: feeling guilty

Guilt is a complex and difficult emotion, especially for young children, who have all the capacity for experiencing guilt, but none of the language with which to rationalise and express what they are feeling

Whilst guilt is unavoidable and can actually serve to help us become more sensitive and responsible people, it is generally regarded as a negative emotion, making it difficult to own and acknowledge. If you are to enable children to explore and deal positively with their feelings of guilt, it is essential that you create a climate where it is acceptable to make mistakes and get things wrong.

For meaningful discussion to take place, adults need to be able to acknowledge their own errors and confront issues in a non-judgmental way. This does not mean condoning unacceptable behaviour or that some behaviours are non-negotiable. You can hear and acknowledge what children are saying without needing to agree with it. Acknowledgement does not equal agreement and it gives you the chance to talk things through. If children feel confident that they will not be judged, they will share their feelings openly and authentically.

Young children learn by listening, watching and copying. If they live in a culture where adults accept responsibility for the things that they have got wrong, then they will learn to do the same, and in so doing, learn that guilt is a perfectly normal human emotion. Your role as practitioner lies in helping children to know the difference between guilt that is 'earned' and guilt that is not, and help them to learn how to respond when they have done something that they later regret.

Using puppets and toys

If you have any large puppets in your setting they can be extremely useful in helping you to explore feelings of guilt. Create simple scenarios within which your puppet characters can do things about which they later feel guilty. The scenarios do not need to be complicated; simply think about the sorts of things that may give rise to guilty feelings for the children in your setting. Here are two scenarios that I have used and found effective.

The sleep-over scenario

Resources: Two large puppets and some plastic creepy crawlies.

I call my characters George and Gloria, but you can use the names of your puppets.

Gloria was very excited because George was coming to stay overnight at her house. He arrived in the afternoon and Gloria enjoyed showing him all her toys and letting him have a ride on her bike. Then they had tea. After they had watched some television, Gloria's mum said it was time for bed.

(You can embellish this part of the story as much as you like, and the children can offer their ideas about how Gloria and George spent the afternoon and what they had to eat.)

They were sent upstairs to get ready for bed and got told off for squealing and bouncing on the beds. Gloria's mum told them to put their night clothes on and have a wash and brush their teeth. George went into the bathroom first and while he was gone Gloria hid a big, plastic spider in his bed. Later, when they were both ready for bed, George pulled back the duvet and saw the massive spider. He thought it was real and burst into tears. Gloria bounced on the bed laughing. Her mother heard the noise and sped upstairs to see what was happening, but by this time George was so upset that he had to be taken home. When Gloria realised what she had done she felt very guilty.

At this point it is also worth talking with the children about other feelings that Gloria may have been experiencing, such as disappointment. She could be angry with herself for having played the trick. In this way, you help children to understand the way in which we often feel a number of emotions all at the same time.

Once you have presented the scenario, you can ask open-ended questions like:

■ How do you think Gloria's mum felt about what had happened?

■ Is there anything that Gloria can do that might make George feel better?

Younger children will enjoy discussing the issues around this scenario, and usually have a wide range of ideas about how it should be resolved. Older children can use the story as a basis for their writing. Through shared writing, for example, they might help Gloria write a letter to George about what has happened and how he/she feels about it.

The broken vase
Here's another scenario to try.

Jake has come round to play at Mina's house. He is very excited because his dad has bought him a new football and he wants to play with it in Mina's back garden. Mina has a massive back garden and her big brother has put up a goal post with a net. Unfortunately, when Jake arrives Mina's dad is in the middle of cutting the grass, so he says that they will need to wait a while before they can play on the lawn.

Mina has been watching a video and wants to see the end of it, but as soon as it is finished she picks up Jake's ball. They begin to pass it to each other across the sitting room and as they get more and more excited Jake trips over the sofa and crashes into the television. The ball flies up into the air and lands on the windowsill, knocking a vase of flowers onto the floor. It is smashed to pieces.

Mina's mum comes rushing in to see what has happened. She is absolutely furious. Mina says that they will clear up the mess. Unfortunately, that does not help Mina's mum to calm down. The vase belonged to her grandmother and was very precious to Mina's mum. She is *very* upset! When they realise what they have done Jake and Mina feel very guilty.

Sharing experiences
You will probably think of many other suitable starting points - breaking someone else's toy, eating someone else's sweets - and once the children have been introduced to such scenarios, they usually find it quite easy to begin to share their own experiences and talk about the things that they have felt guilty about. Encourage them to think about how we might respond when we do things that we later feel sorry for but, most importantly, help them to see that guilt is something that everybody feels and explore the ways in which guilt can be useful in helping us to think about what is right and what is wrong. Support children to understand that we all do things for which we need to say sorry, but that saying sorry is not in itself enough; we have to try hard not to make the same mistake again!

Talk about things that you have done that made you feel guilty. Understanding that the adults they love and respect sometimes feel guilty really helps children to see that guilt is something that we all feel and to realise that the important thing is how we act upon our guilty feelings.

Other activities
■ Share published stories where the characters feel guilty for a variety of reasons, for example *Burglar Bill* by Janet and Allan Ahlberg (Picture Puffin) and *The Teddy Robber* by Ian Beck (Doubleday).

■ Role play and photograph situations that could lead to children feeling guilty. For example:

Somebody about to steal someone else's sweets or crisps;

Somebody breaking someone's model or spoiling somebody's painting;

Somebody about to push someone off a bike.

Look at the photographs with the children and discuss the feelings of the people in the picture.

■ Make a circle and start a tag line, for example 'I felt guilty when ...' (let children pass if they want to.)

■ Share ideas about how to deal with guilty feelings in a positive way, and make a list or a poster representing some of the things we can do when we feel guilty. For example, say sorry, help someone to mend something that is broken, make a card, replace the broken object.

■ With older children, consider things from an alternative point of view. For example, in the story of 'The Billy Goats Gruff', how might the troll have felt about the Billy Goats trip trapping across his bridge? Could Big Billy Goat Gruff have dealt with things another way? Might the Billy Goats have felt guilty about what happened to the troll? (You can do a similar thing with the story of 'The Three Little Pigs': consider how the wolf might have felt and whether the pigs experienced any guilt for how they dealt with the situation!)

Whichever of the activities you decide to try, you will be creating a context within which children can begin to see that while we cannot reverse the things that happen to us, there is no situation that cannot be improved with some reflection and positive thinking.

Exploring emotions:
Feeling jealous

Feelings of jealousy can be powerful and difficult to deal with. The challenge lies in helping children to see that it's okay to be jealous, and that what is important is learning to deal with and express such feelings in ways that do not hurt others

Children as young as three and four are still developing their sense of self. They are affected by the things that happen to them and the ways in which adults respond to these experiences. When young children are feeling jealous, their sense of self, and their security, can be threatened, so it is crucial to think carefully about how you will help them with these strong feelings. They may not even be able to put a name to what they are feeling, and this may make the feelings even more distressing.

If you want to help children explore feeling jealous, you must think about your own feelings about jealousy first. Jealousy is usually seen as a negative emotion, and many of us have been brought up to believe that it is bad to feel jealous. Consequently, many adults try to deny such feelings. When you are looking at jealousy with children, you need to be able to see it as a perfectly normal human emotion that we all experience to varying degrees throughout our lives. The challenge lies in helping children to see that it's okay to be jealous, and that what is important is learning to deal with and express such feelings in ways that do not hurt others.

Jealousy, when it's not properly acknowledged, can turn to anger, resentment or hurt. It will not simply go away, but will stay within us to be triggered at a later date. Unacknowledged jealousy can impair personal development, so if you can help children to acknowledge and deal with their jealous feelings you are doing them a great service.

Using puppets and toys

Most settings have some large puppets, and they can be put to good use when exploring feelings. If you don't have any puppets you can always use teddy bears or soft toys instead. Create simple scenarios within which your characters experience feelings of jealousy. These work best when they are simple everyday events with which the children can identify. The following scenario generally works well as it is one that most young children have experienced.

The new boy

I will call my characters Jake and Mina, but you can substitute the names of your own puppets or toys.

A new boy called Imran has joined Jake and Mina's class. Jake and Mina have been friends for a long time. They play together at home and they play together at nursery/school, but today, something happened that really upset Jake. Mrs Metcalf, their teacher/key worker found him huddled in the book corner in tears.

At first, he was so upset that he could not tell her what was the matter, but after a while he explained that on the way to nursery/school, he and Mina had planned to work together in the construction area to build a robot, but when the time came, Mina said that she didn't want to do that any more. When Jake asked her why she replied that she 'just didn't'. Nothing that Jake said could persuade Mina to work with him on the robot. She told him that she just wanted to go and play outside on the bikes. Jake said that he would go outside too, but Mina said that she wanted to go on her own, so Jake went to the construction area to start work on the robot by himself.
A little later on, he looked out of the window and noticed that Mina was playing on a bike with Imran. He was very, very upset and thought that Mina was not his friend anymore.

Once you have presented the scenario you can use it as a basis for discussion. Ask questions like:

■ Can you think of some words that would describe how Jake is feeling?

■ Is there anything that Mina and Imran could do that might make Jake feel better?

Encourage the children to relate the story to their own experience and, where appropriate, to share their own experiences of feeling jealous. It also helps, where possible, to share your own experiences. When they realise that the adults they like and respect also feel jealous, it really helps them to see that this is a perfectly normal human condition!

A new baby

Perhaps one of the most powerful feelings of jealousy young children experience is after the birth of a baby brother or sister, and this theme can be meaningfully explored through story. One story that I have found particularly useful is *The Very Worst Monster* by Pat Hutchins.

This is a story about a family of monsters and what happens when Billy the baby monster is born. Everyone in the family is convinced that Billy will be the worst monster in the whole world. The only person who disagrees is Billy's big sister, Hazel. As far as she is concerned *she* is the worst monster and she is prepared to go to any lengths to prove it, including trying to get rid of her baby brother! Young children love Hazel's antics and the story provides a useful springboard for an exploration of this issue.

Other useful stories are *Tom and Sam*, also by Pat Hutchins and *John Brown, Rose and the Midnight Cat*, by Jenny Wagner. Many traditional and folk and fairy tales provide rich examples for work about jealousy, for example 'Snow White and the Seven Dwarfs', 'Cinderella' and 'Aladdin'.

Using pictures and photographs

Make a collection of pictures which show children in situations where they may feel jealous. There are several ways of doing this, and once you have made your collection you can use it again and again with different groups of children.

If you or any colleagues are good at drawing, depict a range of scenarios, for example one child receiving a present and other children looking on; someone winning a race with other children coming in behind; a small child looking on as their parents look adoringly at their new baby; two children enjoying a game together with a third child looking on; children in a queue at the ice-cream van and a small child being pulled past it by an adult.

Alternatively, search for pictures in magazines or pose some situations to photograph. With older children, encourage them to see that everyone experiences jealousy differently, and that what makes one person feel jealous may not evoke the same response in their friend.

Making books

With younger children, make a 'We feel jealous when.....' book. Talk with them about the sort of things that cause them to feel jealous and then represent them in a book which can be illustrated with drawings or photographs. If the children pose for the photographs themselves the activity will be much more meaningful to them.

Encourage them to practise facial expressions and think about how their faces and bodies might look when they are feeling jealous.

With older children, support them to make up a story about someone feeling jealous, and help them to role play the story. At intervals in the story 'freeze frame' the action and take photographs. Use the photographs as a basis for a book. The children can dictate the text as a modelled or shared writing experience.

Playing circle games

Sit the children in a circle and pass round a teddy or some other kind of 'talking object.' Explain to the children that only the person holding the talking object can speak and that if they don't want to speak they can 'pass'. Start a tag line, for example 'I feel jealous when ...'

Make a collection of 'desirable' objects and toys and put them in a feely bag. Play some music as you pass a teddy or similar object around the circle. When the music stops, the child with the teddy pulls an item out of the feely bag. The children then imagine that this item is going to be given to their best friend and they will not get one. Would this make them feel jealous or not? This activity helps them to see that we all feel jealous about different things, and that how jealous we feel about something is directly related to how much we would like that thing for ourselves!

Acknowledge children's feelings

All of these activities will help children to begin to understand what can sometimes be confusing and distressing feelings, but it is important to remember that, for very young children, the most powerful learning takes place within the context of their own experience. Therefore, when you notice that someone in your group is experiencing jealousy, pick the right moment and encourage them to talk about the way they are feeling. This will help them to understand that it's okay to feel that way, and once they have done that you may well be able to support them to find ways of dealing with what they are feeling.

In their book *How to Talk So Kids Will Listen and Listen So Kids Will Talk*, Adele Faber and Elaine Mazlish (Piccadilly Press) suggest giving a child his or her wishes in fantasy. For example, when they really, really, want something that you cannot give them, say something like, 'I wish I had the magic power to give you that remote control car.'

Faber and Mazlish explain: 'When children want something they can't have, adults usually respond with logical explanations of why they can't have it. Often the harder we explain, the harder they protest. Sometimes just having someone understand how much you want something makes reality easier to bear.'

This makes such a lot of sense, and over the years I have found this strategy very helpful.

Exploring emotions:
Feeling lonely

We all experience feelings of loneliness and isolation at certain times in our lives. Loneliness can take many forms; it can happen when we are physically separated from our family and friends or when, for whatever reason, we feel on the outside of things

The need to feel loved and accepted is a strong and fundamental human need. We all need to feel part of a group and know that, in whatever way, we can make a personal contribution to that group, but this is not always easy.

For even the most confident and gregarious of us, things can sometimes go out of balance, leaving us with uncomfortable feelings of isolation. When this happens it can feel as if we are the only person in the world that feels this way, and for a young child who has no way of rationalising what is happening to them, these feelings can be extremely distressing. However, through well planned and sensitive work in this area, you can go a long way towards helping children to understand that everyone feels this way some of the time, and not only does this help them as individuals, it also increases their sensitivity to others.

Perhaps one of the most important things you can do is to acknowledge children's feelings of loneliness as they are experiencing them. This helps them to recognise and name what is happening and opens the way for talk and discussion. You can then support them through what they are feeling and develop their understanding further through activities that focus on loneliness.

Using puppets and toys

Find a small soft toy that looks vulnerable, wrap it in a blanket and place it in a bag or box. Explain to the children that you bought the toy in a toy shop because it was sitting all by itself with no other toys to play with. Ask the children to say how they think the toy may be feeling and to make suggestions for ways of helping your toy. A suitable toy never fails to engage the children's emotions and they are usually full of ideas for ways in which they can help.

In the unlikely event that they are not forthcoming, make some suggestions of your own. For example, perhaps you could hold a welcoming party for your toy, find them a special friend, or make them a place to live somewhere in your setting. A simple scenario of this sort is an excellent springboard for promoting discussion about loneliness, and as most children know what it feels like to be lonely, they will readily empathise with your character.

If you have some large puppets in your setting, put them into situations that mirror those experienced by children.

For most young children, one of the most powerful experiences of feeling lonely is when a friend doesn't want to

play with them. Firmly focused on what they want, their friend may be blissfully unaware of how they feel, leaving them feeling even more miserable. The following scenario may prove useful as a way of exploring this issue.

The birthday party scenario

George and Gloria are excited as it's their friend Omar's birthday soon and he is going to have a party. He has told them that there will be a bouncy castle in the back garden and that a magician is going to do tricks for everyone.

George and Gloria spend a long time thinking about what to buy him for a present and finally decide on a football. George's mum takes them to the shop to buy it and they wrap it up (which isn't easy!) ready for the party.

The next day at nursery/school Omar gives out his party invitations, and Gloria is very, very upset when George receives one but she does not. The party is on Saturday, and when George goes to the party Gloria is left at home with no one to play with. She feels very lonely indeed.

Once you have shared this story with the children, ask some open ended questions to get the discussion going. For example:

■ How do you think Gloria was feeling while George was at Omar's party? Can you think of any words that might describe the way she might have felt?

■ Do you think George would have told Gloria about what happened at the party? How might she have felt if he did?

■ Why do you think Gloria was not invited to the party?

■ If you had been George, what might you have done or said to help Gloria feel better?

■ If appropriate, ask the children if anything similar has ever happened to them, and let them share their own experiences. As a follow-up to the discussion, older children might like to use this scenario as a basis for writing experiences.

Using published stories
There are many good stories about loneliness, and some of the best are written by Anthony Browne. In *Willy and Hugh* (Red Fox), Willy is feeling lonely when he meets Hugh. On first appearances they have little in common, but through a process of mutual respect and support, they soon become firm friends, and Hugh no longer feels lonely.

In *Gorilla* (Walker Books), Hannah, the main character, is very lonely indeed. She lives with her father who is always too busy to spend time with her, but when a friendly gorilla takes her on an amazing adventure she stops feeling lonely.

Other excellent books are *Where the Wild Things Are* by Maurice Sendak (Red Fox) and, for younger children in particular, *Hug* by Jez Alborough (Walker Books).

Using visual images
A good way of exploring this issue further would be to contact some relevant charities to ask for posters showing images of loneliness. You might try Help the Aged, the Salvation Army or the Samaritans. Most charities have education officers who are usually happy to help. Visual images can be powerful and the children really enjoy talking about and exploring them. You can also collect and file pictures from newspapers and magazines to use in the same way.

Share your own experiences
Talk with children about times when you have felt lonely and encourage other adults to do the same, as this will really help children to understand that all of us can feel lonely some of the time. Encourage them to share their ideas about situations where people may feel lonely or left out. Start a tag line: 'I feel lonely when.....' and let children talk about the different things that make them feel lonely. Make a list of all the things that come up and see if there are certain things that engender feelings of loneliness more than others. With older children, begin to stretch their thinking by asking them to make suggestions about what they think we can do to help us cope when we feel lonely.

Loneliness is something that none of us can totally avoid, but by carrying out some of the activities described in this article you can go a long way towards helping children to understand loneliness and enable them to see that there are things we can do to help ourselves and others when we do experience such feelings.

Useful addresses
Help the Aged (England)
207-221 Pentonville Road,
London N1 9UZ
Tel: 020 7278 1114
Email: info@helptheaged.org.uk
Website: www.helptheaged.org.uk

Wales
Tel: 02920 346550
Email: infocymru@helptheaged.org.uk

Scotland
Tel: 0131 551 6331
Email: infoscot@helptheaged.org.uk

Northern Ireland
Tel: 02890 230 666
Email: infoni@helptheaged.org.uk

The Salvation Army
101 Newington Causeway
London SE1 6BN
Tel: 020 7367 4500
Email: thq@salvationarmy.org.uk
Website: www.salvationarmy.org.uk

Samaritans
The Upper Mill
Kingston Road
Ewell
Surrey KT17 2AF
Tel: 020 8394 8300
Email: admin@samaritans.org
Website: www.samaritans.org

Useful resources
An excellent resource for exploring this issue is Flip the Bear. Flip is a bear who lives on a ship that is travelling around the world. The only trouble is that he needs to go to a nursery/school and they do not have one on the ship. So his mum and dad decide that he should leave the ship and go to school. Flip can go into any early years setting and he takes his camera and notebook with him to record his adventures. Although he is excited about this, when he finally leaves his mum and dad he is very lonely. The children look after him until it is time for him to return to the ship. Flip is available from Lawrence Educational Publications (01922 643833) and comes with an explanatory booklet and a video showing how he has been used in two early years settings.

Another useful resource is the video *Angel and Friends* (available from the same source). This is a collection of ten stories told with the help of large puppets, where the theme of loneliness appears in a variety of contexts that are familiar to young children.

Family Album: This is a set of 32 colour photos that can be used to support discussions on families. (Available from Development Education Centre, Birmingham; Telephone: 0121 472 3255.)

Exploring emotions:
Feeling excited

Excitement can be a shared experience or one that is intensely personal, and what excites one person will not necessarily excite another

Excitement can be experienced in a variety of ways, and for very young children it can be an emotion that they find difficult to deal with. Sometimes, the feelings of excitement can be so intense that they tip over into quite a different emotion, for example becoming so overwhelmed with excitement at their birthday party that they end up bursting into tears!

In some situations, such as looking forward to going on holiday, excitement builds up over time, at other times it may happen almost instantly in response to an unexpected event. Either way, it varies in intensity. It may take the form of a pleasant feeling of anticipation or it may be so powerful that we feel we will explode, and there are many variables in between.

Excitement can be a shared experience or one that is intensely personal, and what excites one person will not necessarily excite another. Excitement is a complex emotion, but by spending some time exploring it, you can enhance children's awareness of their own feelings and enable them to understand others more fully.

Using puppets and toys

If you have a favourite teddy or soft toy, tell children that he or she is excited. Write a letter to your toy explaining that they are going to be taken on a wonderful holiday by a relative. Encourage the children to speculate about why the toy is excited and all the things that they might be looking forward to. Use this as a springboard for getting them to discuss the things that excite them and share situations where they have felt excited.

If you have some large puppets, put them into story scenarios that mirror the situations the children get excited about, for example a trip to a theme park or going to a friend's birthday party. Encourage them to talk about events that have taken place in your setting about which they have felt excited - a picnic, a special visitor, a celebration - and all the time, encourage them to notice the way in which not everybody is excited about the same thing.

To help them to understand this you may like to try out the following story scenario.

The performance scenario

All of the children have been busy making plans for a special coffee morning for their parents and carers, who have been invited to spend the morning at nursery/school. They have planned what sort of cakes they will make and as part of the celebrations they are going to put on a performance of all the songs and stories they have learned throughout the year.

Gloria is really excited about this and is desperate to play the part of Goldilocks in 'Goldilocks and the Three Bears.' At first, George says that he does not want to be in it, but Gloria persuades him to be Daddy Bear! She says it will be lots of fun and that they can practise at home.

Gloria has lots of words to learn, but she isn't a bit bothered and learns them quickly. Her mum has made her a special costume and she is so excited she just can't wait for the day of the coffee morning to arrive.

George, on the other hand, is uncertain and nervous about the whole thing. He can't seem to remember what he has to say and he doesn't like dressing up as Daddy Bear.

The day before the coffee morning, Gloria is so excited she can hardly keep still, and barely seems to hear when George tells her that he is scared about the next day.

Gloria tells him that it will be really good and that he shouldn't be scared. However, when the next day comes and everyone is getting ready for the performance, George bursts into tears and runs into the toilet. Someone else has to be found to play the part of Daddy Bear.

Gloria really enjoys herself playing the part of Goldilocks and smiles from ear to ear when the performance is over and everyone applauds.

Once you have shared this scenario with the children, encourage them to think about why the two characters responded so differently, and help them to understand the ways in which we are all excited by different things.

Start a 'tag line'. Sit the children in a circle and begin by saying: 'I feel excited when ...' By sharing your own experiences with the children you will encourage them to talk more freely, and anyone who feels they don't want to say anything can pass. When everyone has had their say, you can then offer the children who have passed another opportunity to take part. It may just be that they needed more time to think.

Using published stories
There are a wide variety of published stories that can help you to explore excitement. Although somewhat seasonal, *The Snowman* by Raymond Briggs (Picture Puffin) has to be one of the best! When the small boy in the story wakes up to find the entire landscape covered with snow, his sense of excitement is almost unrivalled. Share this story with children and encourage them to talk about times when they may have experienced the same feeling.

For younger children, *Dear Daddy* by Philippe Dupasquier (Andersen Press) is an excellent book. Sophie, the main character, writes to her father who is away at sea, telling him about all the exciting things that happen every day. She makes lots of suggestions for all the things they will be able to do together when he comes home, and her excitement when he finally arrives home is beautifully depicted through the sensitive illustrations. In *So Much* by Trish Cooke (Walker Books), the whole family are excited to be together for Dad's birthday party.

For older children, *At the Crossroads* by Rachel Isadora (Red Fox) is a lovely story about a group of children who live in a South African shanty town and are waiting for their fathers to return from working in the mines. The author conveys the children's excitement at the forthcoming reunion with great success and in a way that young children can easily relate to.

Working with images
Collect pictures from magazines, brochures

and old calendars of people who look excited. Use these as a basis for discussion, encouraging children to offer their opinions about why they think the people are excited. Include some pictures of people who do not look excited. Invite children to sort them out and encourage them to give reasons why they have sorted them in the way that they have.

Carry out a survey
Make a list of all the adults that work in your setting and let children talk to them about the things that they find exciting. This is a really good way of helping children to understand that what is exciting for one person may not be exciting for another.

To build on this activity, make a list/have a range of pictures of exciting things to do and get children to choose which one they would do if they could only choose one. With older children you could graph the results as part of your work for Mathematical Development.

Make an excitement-o-meter
All you need is a piece of card which depicts a continuum from not very exciting to very exciting indeed! There will need to be some kind of dial or indicator that the children can move to show how excited they would be by a given event. Once you have created your 'excitement-o-meter', suggest a range of activities and get the children to indicate how exciting they would find them by moving the dial.

Hold a photographic exhibition
Ask children (and adults) to bring in photographs of themselves doing something that they found really exciting. Display the photographs where they can be easily seen by the children and use as a basis for discussion. This is an excellent activity to stimulate speaking and listening and never fails to engage children's interest.

Excitement can sometimes be such an intense emotion that it is difficult to contain, and many of the children will have heard adults telling them that they have got 'overexcited,' so it would also be worthwhile to spend some time discussing occasions when this can happen. In this way, you can help young children to learn more about emotions and build on their self-knowledge.

EXPLORING EMOTIONS 21

Exploring emotions:
Feeling proud

Pride can be experienced in different ways, but whether a shared or a personal experience, private or public, by exploring this emotion with children you will enhance their understanding of themselves and others

Feeling proud of ourselves as a result of something we have achieved is important for all of us, and especially important for young children. They are at a crucial time in their lives; a time when they are forming opinions about who they are and how they fit into the world around them, and attitudes formed at this stage are likely to stay with them.

To feel proud involves us in experiencing a sense of honour and self-respect; a sense of personal worth. It enables us to take pleasure in our own or somebody else's achievements, and as such is inextricably linked to the development of self-esteem. For this reason, it is extremely important that you devote time and attention to the ways in which you enable young children to experience this important emotion.

Celebrating children's achievements

All the time you are working with children you are consciously or unconsciously supporting them to feel proud of their accomplishments, but when an early years team devotes a little time and attention to considering exactly how they do this, they do it even better.

The way in which you give feedback to children about what they have achieved can have a massive impact on the way they feel about themselves, so you need to think really carefully about how you do this. We all need recognition for the things we have done, but the most important thing we can do is to help children think well of themselves, so that their feelings of pride are genuinely their own. Praise can have negative implications; in your attempts to make children feel good about themselves you can inadvertently undermine their capacity to feel proud themselves.

In simple terms, unless you are thoughtful about the way you respond to children, it is all too easy to turn them into 'praise junkies'. You can actually make them dependent on your approval and take away their power to evaluate their own efforts. For this reason, it is really important that you develop encouragement strategies. This means that you must work hard at being descriptive rather than evaluative and acknowledge children's work and ideas by

making specific comments. You must develop the skill of asking open-ended questions, and encourage children to describe their efforts, ideas and products. In short, you must develop their capacity to express for themselves the things they feel proud about.

Using photographs

When you talk with children about the things they have achieved you can introduce the word 'proud', and suggest that in order to celebrate their achievement

22 EXPLORING EMOTIONS

you might take a photograph of what they have done. Once you have trained them to use a camera they can take the photograph themselves. These photographs can then be displayed in a special 'Things we are proud of' book or on a special display board where there is a place for every child to have a picture of something they are proud of. If the thing they are proud of cannot be photographed children can dictate the story of what they are feeling proud about. Encourage adults in your setting to contribute to the display, and to talk to children about the things they feel proud about.

Using puppets and toys

If you have a favourite teddy or soft toy, tell children that he or she is feeling proud about something they have done. Explain that your character has done something to help someone, and that they feel really proud about it. You could even introduce another toy to represent the one that has been helped. Tell children that one toy was crying because they had no-one to play with, or because someone was doing something unkind to them. Encourage children to generate ideas for how the other toy may have helped, and use this as a springboard for getting them to talk about times when they have felt proud about the things they have done. Simple scenarios like this help children to understand that you can feel proud for lots of different reasons.

If you have some large puppets, put them into situations that mirror the challenges children have to deal with, and explore the feelings of pride that are experienced when challenges are overcome. You may like to try the following story scenario.

Jake feels proud

Jake's mum tells him that a letter has come to say that he needs to go to the dentist's for a check-up. Jake is frightened and does not want to go.

He tells his friend Mina about how he feels. Mina says that she never minds going to see the dentist, and tells Jake that if he is brave and goes for his check-up she will buy him a present.

Jake says that he will try to be brave, and his mum rings up to make an appointment for him.

Once he has been to see the dentist, Jake feels really proud of himself, and his mum and Mina tell him that they also feel proud about what he has done. Jake tells Mina all about the filling he had and then asks Mina if she has bought him the present that she promised him.

Mina hands Jake an envelope, and inside the envelope there is a really special toothbrush. Each time Jake uses it he feels proud about going to see the dentist, even though he felt frightened.

Once you have shared this scenario with the children, encourage them to think about the way in which Jake and Mina felt differently about going to the dentist's. Talk about whether Mina had done anything that she could feel proud about.

Start a 'tag line'. Sit the children in a circle and begin by saying: 'I feel proud when ....' share your own experiences with the children, and encourage them to tell everyone about something they have felt proud about.

Using pictures and posters

Another good way to explore this emotion is by cutting pictures from magazines and collecting posters of individuals and groups of people who are feeling proud of themselves. You can then make a display and invite the children to offer suggestions for why the people may be feeling proud. You might have a picture of a climber who has just reached a summit, a football team that has just scored a goal or won a match, a mother with a new baby or a child holding their new puppy. Once you start hunting you'll be amazed how many pictures you will find, and if you get the children and parents hunting too, you'll soon have a good collection.

You could also make a collection of medals, certificates and cups and explore why they might have been presented. This sort of activity helps children to understand that feelings of pride can be experienced in a variety of contexts.

To help children understand that different people feel proud about different things, collect pictures of different people or groups of people, for example a jockey, an athlete, a postman or woman, a police officer, a gardener, a mum, a dad, a grandma or grandad, a choir or a football team. Encourage children to think about things that may make them feel proud, and be prepared to challenge stereotypes - the grandma may be very proud because she has just learned to ride a motorbike!

In common with many other emotions, feelings of pride can be full of subtlety and complexity, but by beginning to explore such feelings at an early age you can really help children towards a better understanding of both themselves and others.

Using published stories

There are numerous published stories about children who feel proud about things they have done, but the Alfie stories by Shirley Hughes are among the best.

In *Alfie's Feet* (Red Fox), Alfie is so proud of his new wellingtons, and in *Alfie Gives a Hand*, Alfie overcomes his own fears in order to help another child.

Lucy's Picture by Nicola Moon (Orchard Books) is also an excellent book for exploring feelings of pride.

Exploring emotions: feeling irritable

A feeling that may start out as frustration can quickly become irritability. With a little careful thought, you can lead children (and yourself!) towards a greater level of understanding and self-knowledge

We all feel irritable from time to time, but this is a difficult emotion for children to understand. As adults, we are usually, although not always, able to rationalise and find reasons for our feelings of irritability, which at least goes some way to helping us cope with what we are feeling. For children, who have not yet developed this ability, such feelings can be uncomfortable and distressing.

However, by giving this emotion a little time and attention you can help children to deal with their feelings more effectively and make sure that the feelings do not spiral downwards into even more extreme feelings. Irritability is a subtle emotion; less extreme than anger or sadness, but without acknowledgement it can soon turn into anger or distress.

When we're feeling irritable we can be short-tempered and easily annoyed, and whilst we find this state easy to understand in adults, we are often far less tolerant and understanding when children are irritable. It is as if we do not expect children to experience this emotion!

It is also interesting to explore the ways in which irritability can often be traced back to quite precise human dilemmas. The cause could be physical, like feeling unwell or being unable to meet a physical challenge. It could result from feeling jealous or inadequate, or it may be because we feel that we are not equal to an intellectual challenge, such as not knowing the answer to a question or being unable to work something out.

A feeling may start out as frustration, but move on to become irritability. With a little careful thought, you can lead children (and yourself!) towards a greater level of understanding and self-knowledge.

Acknowledging feelings

Young children find it difficult to understand abstract concepts, so they will find irritability far easier to recognise if it is acknowledged when it is happening. Next time you feel irritable or short-tempered, think about whether it would be worth sharing your feelings with the children! Tell them that you feel irritable and explain why. It may be that the baby kept you awake all night or your car broke down on the way to work. When children appear to be irritable, talk with them about their feelings and their reasons for feeling that way.

Empathise with how they are feeling, even if they cannot explain why. It is all too easy to try to distract a child from the way they

'Next time you feel irritable or short-tempered, think about whether it would be worth sharing your feelings with the children! Tell them that you feel irritable and explain why.'

are feeling in an attempt to get them to 'snap out of it', but by talking with them about how they are feeling you expand their vocabulary of feeling words and help them to understand themselves better. You also help them to see that everyone feels irritable from time to time, and that it is nothing to feel guilty about.

Using puppets and toys

Using a puppet or a toy to explore irritability enables children to think, reason and apply what they have learned from experience in a context where they are not feeling irritable themselves. Think up some simple scenarios that mirror the things that lead to irritability in children and use them as a springboard for discussion. You might like to try the following scenario.

Gloria at bedtime

Gloria was excited because her aunty and uncle were coming to tea. She could hardly wait for them to arrive but she enjoyed herself helping her mum to get the tea ready.

When she heard the car pull up outside she ran to the gate to meet her aunty and uncle and they all played in the garden until it was time to eat.
After tea, Gloria's Uncle Jo read her some stories and then her mum told her it was time for bed.

Gloria didn't want to go to bed and begged for one more story, and then one more, until finally her mum said she must go to bed. Reluctantly, Gloria went upstairs to get ready for bed and her mum tucked her up and then went downstairs, but Gloria couldn't go to sleep!

First she got up and went downstairs saying she was thirsty. Later, she got up saying that she had a stomach ache. Then she got up again to say that there was a spider in her bedroom. By the time it was midnight and her uncle and aunty had gone home Gloria was still awake.

When morning came she did not want to get up for nursery/school, did not want to get dressed and she would not eat her breakfast! She was so tired and irritable, that her mum had to almost drag her to school.

When she got to school her friends wanted to talk to her and show her things but Gloria wasn't interested. She did not feel like playing with anyone, and when it was time to sing she refused to join in. After singing Gloria tried to build a house with Lego, but when it wouldn't work out she threw the Lego on the floor and stormed off to the book corner. Ten minutes later her friends found her curled up fast asleep in the book corner.

Once you have shared this scenario with the children, you can use it as the basis for a discussion. Ask questions to start things off. For example:

- Why do you think Gloria kept getting out of bed?

- Why do you think she was so irritable in the morning?

- How do you think Gloria's mum felt about the way she was behaving?

- How do you think the other children felt about how she behaved?

- What do you think will happen when Gloria wakes up?

Encourage children to relate the story to their own experience by asking them if they have ever felt the same way as Gloria. Spend a little time thinking about the ways in which people behave when they feel irritable, for example being snappy and short-tempered, being rude to people, not wanting to join in and finding it difficult to concentrate.

Share your own experiences
Talk with children about the things that make you feel irritable and encourage the other adults in your setting to do the same. You might consider making a book or a pictorial display. Collect photographs of adults and children and by the side of the photographs record the things that make them feel irritable. This will help children to understand that there are some things that cause irritation to us all, but that sometimes what irritates one person will not necessarily irritate another.

Using visual images
It is amazing how many pictures you can find in newspapers and magazines of both children and adults looking irritated! Make a collection of these pictures and encourage children to speculate about why the people in the photographs might be irritated. Mix the pictures up with others that depict different kinds of feelings, and let the children sort them out. With younger children, take photographs of some of the adults in your setting looking

Using published stories
There are examples of people feeling irritable in many published stories, but one that is extremely useful is *The Good Mood Hunt* by Hiawyn Oram and Joanne Partis (OUP). In this story Hannah, the main character, wakes up feeling really happy, but becomes very irritable when she remembers that she has nothing to show in 'show and tell'. Encouraged by her father, she sets off to hunt for her good mood, which returns when she has found the things she wants for the show and tell session. As you explore this text, draw children's attention to the illustrations and get them to notice the way in which Hannah's expressions and body language change with her changing moods.

Other useful texts for work in this area are *The Bad Tempered Ladybird* by Eric Carle (Puffin) and *Where the Wild Things Are* by Maurice Sendak (Red Fox).

As a way of exploring the ways in which adults feel irritated you might read *Not Now, Bernard!* by David McKee (Red Fox) or *It was Jake!* by Anita Jeram (Walker). Talk with children about why they think the adults in these stories look and feel irritated. If you feel brave enough, get the children to identify the times when they have noticed *you* feeling irritated!

irritated, for example when the children haven't put things away properly or when they have left the taps running! Once you put your mind to it you will be able to think of a whole host of reasons for being irritated!

Irritation is not an easy emotion to deal with, as it is subtler than the more extreme feelings of anger or jealousy, so for this reason, it is probably best to leave focusing directly on it until you have developed the children's understanding of the more straightforward feelings.

Exploring emotions: feeling hopeful

Hope is about expectation. It is really important that you help children to have high expectations, and by explicitly focusing on this most important feeling, you can help them to do just that

Hope is such a positive emotion, and one with which all young children will be familiar, even if they are unable to put a name to it! When they want to go outside to play, they hope that it will not rain (especially if they are not allowed out in the rain). When their birthday is approaching, they hope for that much sought after present, and when it's nearly time for them to go on holiday, they hope that the days will pass quickly. They hope there will be sand to dig in, water to splash in and a theme park with rides! They may also know what it feels like to have their hopes dashed.

However, this is not about disappointment, it's about feeling hopeful, and as such, it is one of the most satisfying of emotions to explore with children. You will probably find that as you do so, you share many of the things that the children hope for, and this makes it even more exciting. When you plant seeds, you hope they will grow. When you plan a picnic, a visit or a party, you hope that everyone will have a really good time, and when you watch a football match, you hope that your team will win. Hope is about expectation, and it is really important that you help children to have high expectations, and by explicitly focusing on this most important feeling, you can help them to do just that.

Using puppets and toys
If you have any large puppets, tell some simple story scenarios that focus on feeling hopeful. They do not need to be complicated. In fact, the simplest ones are usually the most effective as children find them easy to relate to. Simply think about the things that make the children in your setting feel hopeful, and base your stories on those things. You may like to try out the following scenario.

The lost puppy
George and Gloria were in the park with George's dad. After they had played on the swings, the slide and the climbing frame and fed the ducks on the lake, George said he wanted to play football. Luckily, his Dad had bought a football with him so they ran over to the grass to start the game.

George and Gloria kicked the ball backwards and forwards to each other, and then George's dad gave the ball such a big kick that it soared over to the other side of the park. George and Gloria raced off after the ball, and it was then that they saw the little puppy. It was running about by some bushes.

'Talk with them about how they want their model, picture or construction to turn out. Celebrate with them when their hopes come to fruition and support them when they do not.'

When it saw George and Gloria it bounded up to them and started to jump up and lick them. They looked around the park to see if they could see who it belonged to but there was hardly anyone about. They looked to see if it had a collar on with a name and address, but it didn't.

George's dad said that it was time to go home for tea. George really liked the puppy and thought it was too little to be left on its own. He pleaded and pleaded with his dad to let him take it home. In the end, his dad gave in and said they would

26 EXPLORING EMOTIONS

> 'When you plant seeds, you hope they will grow. When you plan a picnic, a visit or a party, you hope that everyone will have a really good time, and when you watch a football match, you hope that your team will win.'

take it home until they found out who it belonged to.

George was so happy. He hoped and hoped that he would be able to keep the puppy.

Use this story as a springboard for discussing hope. Encourage the children to think about how George was feeling and let them share their own experiences of times when they have really hoped that something would turn out a certain way.

Using published stories
There are many published stories featuring hopeful characters. For younger children, try *Hug* by Jez Alborough (Walker Books). In this story, a little chimp looks for someone to give him a hug. He tries and tries, without success, but he never gives up hope, and is eventually rewarded when he finds his mother.

Another very good story is *Little Bear's Special Wish* by Gillian Lobel (Little Tiger Press). In this story Little Bear wants to give his mummy the most special birthday present in the world. He wants to give her a star, and he stops at nothing until he is able to find one.

But perhaps the ultimate in hopeful stories is *Goodbye Mog* by Judith Kerr (Picture Lions). In this story Mog dies but, as the family weeps, a little bit of Mog stays awake to see what will happen next! The rest of the book sees Mog looking on as the family get a new kitten. The kitten is the only one that can see Mog, who takes the little kitten under her wing until it has settled into the family. When she is satisfied that the little kitten can cope on its own, Mog flies up and up, right into the sun. This is a really triumphant book, and along with the other two, gives children really powerful messages without us needing to spell them out.

Share experiences
Tell children about the things that you hope for and encourage your colleagues to do the same. This is a really good way to show children that sometimes we hope for things that we want for ourselves but that it is also important to hope for things that will be of benefit to others.

Make your desires into a book or have a 'Gallery of hope' where each child's hopes are displayed alongside their photograph.

Make a 'Guess what I am hoping for' book. Have a page for each child where you display their photograph and a picture of what they are hoping for. Cover the picture with a flap and let the other children guess what they have hoped for. If they have difficulty with this concept, contextualise it for them by framing it in a little story. Get them to imagine that they are going to get a present and encourage them to think about what they hope it will be. You might even wrap something up in a box and get them to say what they hope will be inside.

Play circle games
Sit children in a circle and begin a tag line: 'My name is .... and I hope we can play ...... today', or 'My name is .... and I hope I will get .... for my birthday'.

Collect pictures and photographs of people looking hopeful. Pass them around the circle and encourage children to speculate about what the person may be hoping for.

With older children, encourage them to put themselves in someone else's shoes, for example their mum or dad, or a brother or sister. Get them to think about what the hopes of these other people might be.

Share children's hopes
When children are engaged in their own self-initiated activities, this is an excellent time to discuss what they are hoping for. Talk with them about how they want their model, picture or construction to turn out. Celebrate with them when their hopes come to fruition and support them when they do not. Such times present a crucial opportunity for learning, and enable you to help children to see that we can retain our hope even when things don't work out the way we want them to.

If you do this well, you help children to understand that there is no such thing as failure. You help them to see that what they have got is a result, and that if they don't like the result they have got, they can change what they do until they get the result that they want.

This is one of the most precious gifts you can give them. By helping them to understand this, you lay the foundations for deep-seated hope, and when a child has this, their lives will be so much richer.

EXPLORING EMOTIONS 27

How to help your child
handle their emotions

There is no magic recipe to help your child be happy but parents who talk to their child and listen to their emotional messages, celebrate happiness in themselves and their child, provide the kind of 'emotional coaching' which is invaluable

Before children can learn to control their emotions they need to know how to name and recognise their emotions. Sharing a family album or magazine pictures and discussing the faces and expressions can be a valuable experience. Children are fascinated by pictures and photographs of people and they can spend long periods of time poring over them and making sense of them.

Cut out pictures from magazines together and talk about how the person in the picture is feeling and why they may be feeling the way they do. Remember, you know your child best. You can read their emotional state from their facial expressions and body language. Often you just know how your child is feeling even when they can't find the words to tell you.

Feeding back on the non-verbal behaviours you notice can also be valuable. 'I noticed you frowning - are you feeling worried?' (rather than 'You're frowning - you must be worried') 'I heard you stamping upstairs - is there anything wrong?' (rather than 'Why are you so mad?')

Children should have the right to express both positive and negative emotions in an assertive manner. To do so can improve their confidence in themselves and in the relationships they form throughout life.

Children who are supported by people who love them are better at handling their own emotions, are more effective at soothing themselves when upset and get upset less often. Their stress levels are low, they are in better physical health, have fewer behaviour problems and are more popular with their classmates.

Caroline McAdam

Here is something for your kitchen wall:

Children learn what they live

If a child lives with criticism, he learns to condemn.

If a child lives with hostility, he learns to fight.

If a child lives with ridicule, he learns to be shy.

If a child lives with shame, he learns to feel guilty.

If a child lives with tolerance, he learns to be patient.

If a child lives with encouragement, he learns confidence.

If a child lives with praise, he learns to appreciate.

If a child lives with fairness, he learns justice.

If a child lives with security, he learns to have faith.

If a child lives with approval, he learns to like himself.

If a child lives with acceptance and friendship, he learns to find love in the world.

PHOTOCOPY THIS PAGE TO GIVE TO PARENTS

28 **EXPLORING EMOTIONS**